CONVERSATIONS ABOUT THE MEANING OF LIFE

DAVID BENATAR
THADDEUS METZ

INTERVIEWED BY

JASON WERBELOFF
MARK OPPENHEIMER

OBSIDIAN WORLDS PUBLISHING

Conversations about the Meaning of Life
Copyright: Jason Keith Werbeloff, Mark Oppenheimer,
David Benatar, and Thaddeus Metz
Editors: Yolande Coetser and David Christianson
Publisher: Obsidian Worlds Publishing
Published: 25 June 2021

CONTENTS

PREFACE

Jason Werbeloff's first encounter with Professor Metz, who immediately insisted he refer to him as 'Thad', was in his second year as a Philosophy student.

Thad's teaching style in those classes was as affable and accessible as he is. Most of each session was spent prying objections and responses from his students to key arguments. Everything was up for debate. Each premise was interrogated – and no objection was unwelcome.

Thad's dialectic style of practising Philosophy never left him. It informed the lectures Jason gave years later to his own students, and more recently, the *Brain in a Vat* Philosophy YouTube channel Mark Oppenheimer and Jason run.

While Jason was studying Philosophy under Thad, Mark studied ethics with Professor Benatar at the University of Cape Town. Students would marvel at his ability to remember the hundreds of students in his class by name, while facilitating a philosophical dialogue between them. Professor Benatar's willingness to engage controversial ideas in the relentless pursuit of truth is a rare virtue which has inspired Mark to adopt a similar approach in his work as an Advocate.

Both writers are regarded as titans in the field of the meaning of life. Professor Metz's book, *Meaning in Life,* and Professor Benatar's books, *Better Never to Have Been* and *The Human Predicament*, are crucial to the debates in this area.

This book is conducted in the Socratic style of both professors. Their books on the subject are superb, but rather than providing you with essays on their views on the meaning of life, we invited Professors Benatar and

Metz to have a conversation with us.

And with each other.

We begin with Professor Benatar's view, that the capacity for humans to have meaningful lives is severely limited. Although it might at first glance appear that we have meaningful lives, this is only the case from our human perspective.

Once we expand that perspective to a cosmic view, our lives are largely meaningless. Humans make almost no impact on the larger universe – and this cosmic perspective also matters.

Professor Metz is more optimistic. Living a meaningful life, on his view, is achieved through the combination of three features: the good, the beautiful, and the true. Humans, Professor Metz argues, are capable of obtaining enough of each of these three values to live meaningful lives.

Professor Metz rejects Professor Benatar's position. He offers two objections – that the human perspective matters over the cosmic perspective, and there is an incoherence in Professor Benatar's view. Professor Benatar responds in the postscripts.

The time we spent discussing these issues with Professors Benatar and Metz was enormously meaningful for us.

We like to imagine that even from a cosmic perspective, these conversations matter.

Jason Werbeloff and Mark Oppenheimer
May 2021

THE MEANING OF LIFE:
DAVID BENATAR

DAVID BENATAR

You are probably familiar with the myth of Sisyphus, who was punished by the gods by being forced to roll a rock up a hill. When he got it to the top, it would just roll down, and he would once again have to roll it to the top. He was doomed to perform this boring and repetitive task endlessly for the rest of eternity.

This myth makes its way into a paper by Richard Taylor, who imagines a twist in the story – namely that the gods show mercy and implant in Sisyphus a desire to endlessly roll rocks. The question is what this would do to his predicament? Would it relieve it entirely? Would it mitigate it somewhat? Would it make no difference?

JASON WERBELOFF

Does the Sisyphus who now wants to roll a rock up the hill suddenly think his life is meaningful? Is your life meaningful if, subjectively, you think it is?

DAVID BENATAR

That is one of the great divides in debates about what counts as meaning in life. There are two sides: a subjectivist school and an objectivist view. Subjectivists think that meaning really consists in your feeling that your life is meaningful. Objectivists, on the other hand, think that this is not enough, and your life has to meet some objective conditions if it is to be meaningful. Of course, objectivists acknowledge that people can feel that their lives are meaningful, but objectivists would say that feeling meaningful is not the same as being meaningful. A person's life might feel meaningful and meet the objective conditions for meaningfulness; it might feel meaningful and not meet the objective conditions; it might not feel meaningful and yet meet the objective conditions; or it might neither feel meaningful nor meet the objective conditions.

MARK OPPENHEIMER

Thad Metz, in his book *Meaning in Life*, makes a full-frontal assault on this subjectivist view. A lot of people intuitively opt for the notion that 'whatever you say is meaningful in life - is meaningful; the differences are just a matter of the individual's particular conception of it'. Metz starts by listing behaviours where people have (or could have) claimed to be performing a meaningful activity. These include keeping a precise number of hairs on their head, standing in queues compulsively, counting blades of grass, eating their own feces, and repeatedly re-watching episodes of *Buffy the Vampire Slayer*. He argues that even if the person enjoys this activity – and claims they find it meaningful – that does not make it so. You cannot convert these essentially meaningless activities into something which is actually meaningful.

DAVID BENATAR

Here Thad Metz uses a common argumentative technique, namely to point to examples where it is counter-intuitive to suggest that an activity is meaningful, even though the person engaged in those activities insists they are. This is meant to count against the subjectivist view. That's one kind of argument and it's one to which I am sympathetic. It does seem to me that the meaning of life is something about which you can be mistaken. We can be mistaken about most things, but not everything. You might not be able to be mistaken about whether you exist, or whether you are currently in pain, but you can be mistaken about whether your life is meaningful.

Another way to argue against subjectivism is to ask what you mean when you ask, 'does my life have meaning?' There is a lot of disagreement about that question; some thinkers want to specify some necessary and sufficient conditions for what it would take for life to be meaningful. I'm not personally optimistic that that sort of project could be successful. I don't think that we are dealing with a subject matter that lends itself to that level of precision. But I do think we know roughly what it is we are speaking about when people ask whether their lives have meaning. They are asking: Is there some point to all of this? Is there some purpose to it? Is my life significant in some way? These are not exactly the same thing, but they are all in a family of connected ideas. I think that is the sort of thing that people are asking when they wonder whether their lives have meaning. It is difficult to see counting blades of grass as actually providing purpose, or making one's life significant, no matter how much a subject might think it does.

Jason Werbeloff

Let me put you on the spot and ask, what do you think the answer is? Do you think people's lives have meaning?

David Benatar

There are different perspectives from which you could ask that question. Lives do or can contain some meaning, but no lives contain other sorts of quite important forms of meaning.

If you understand 'meaning' as significance or purpose, there are a variety of ways in which this might apply to your life. You might be of significance to the members of your family – your very being may matter to them. The activities that you engage in may have a positive impact or, indeed, a negative impact on them. Thus, your life could have meaning from the perspective of your family. I think there are vast numbers of people – not everybody, sadly – whose lives have meaning from that perspective. We can shift from there to a broader perspective. If you go beyond the family to larger communities, again we find that many people have an impact or significance, and could credibly say their lives have meaning from that perspective. From a yet broader perspective – the perspective of all humanity – far fewer lives could be said to have meaning. Most people go through their life without having a significant impact, if viewed from the perspective of humanity as a whole. Somebody, for example, who invented a vaccine for COVID would have an impact on humanity at large. That would be a life that is significant from that perspective. But finally, there's the broadest perspective of all – what is often called the cosmic perspective – and the question is, could any human's life have meaning from that perspective? This is where I'm very pessimistic. I don't think that our lives do have meaning at this broadest level. Some disagree – and we should talk about what they think the cosmic meaning might be – but my view is that they fall short. Given that cosmic meaning is, in a sense, the ultimate form of meaning, that news is going to be somewhat disappointing for many people.

JASON WERBELOFF

Why do you think that the cosmic sense of meaning is 'the ultimate form of meaning'? Why is the most important sense of meaning not at the individual level? Or even at a community level? Why would that sort of grander scale be more important?

DAVID BENATAR

In general, the broader the perspective, the more the meaning it has on one axis. Not, of course, on all axes (or dimensions) but there is an axis on which the broader the perspective, the more meaning you have. Think about what generates this sort of question. Imagine you get up in the morning and you eat and clean yourself and get ready to go to work in a normal world. Then you go out there and deal with all the frustrations of work and earn your living. Why are you doing all this? At one level, it is so that you can eat and keep yourself alive so that you can continue doing the work that you're doing. At some point people will step back and will wonder what the point of all of this is. If you layer in all the suffering that people have in their lives, the struggles that they have to endure and the hardships of life, it's very reasonable to ask, 'what is this all about? What's the point of all of this?' And if the point is just that I'm giving you some meaning and you're giving me some meaning, it looks like a closed circle. It has a certain element of value to it, but it doesn't look like it's enough to justify all the hardships, the strivings, the struggle, and, of course, ultimately the death.

MARK OPPENHEIMER

There are two different points here. One is that there might be small amounts of meaning in our lives but a lot of people really are engaged in a Sisyphean task. Their lives are highly repetitive and are often filled with other sorts of misery. That small meaning isn't going to do much to offset the bad stuff. The other point is a perspective issue. It may be that some great people – like Martin Luther King or Julius Caesar – are going to have a huge impact for generations, maybe even thousands of years. But once we zoom out and consider how briefly humanity has existed, compared to all of time and all of space, it starts to look entirely insignificant. So, one might say that if life has some level of meaning, it's only on a micro-level. Once we zoom out, life might as well never have been because it seems so totally insignificant and meaningless.

DAVID BENATAR

Think about two children squabbling in the sandpit. From their perspective, whatever it is that they're bickering about is of immense significance, important enough for them to be coming to blows perhaps. But if you just step back a few yards, it looks a lot less important. And if you step back to view the whole of the world, that little squabble going on in the sandpit is utterly insignificant.

JASON WERBELOFF

But why do we think the viewpoint of those children in the sandpit is less important than the cosmic view? Perhaps it's because we do have cosmic significance? I can think of one way in which this might be the case; when we create something beautiful, like art perhaps or a gorgeous mathematical proof. When we do that, are we not contributing to something that seems to be outside of time and place? If, for example, you sculpt a magnificent statue, it appears, to me, to have greater value than the mere clay it is made out of. It seems like you have created something new in the world. And the amount of beauty in the universe has increased and not just in one tiny corner of the planet earth.

DAVID BENATAR

I'm not sure I agree. You've heard the phrase that beauty is in the eye of the beholder? That usually means one thing, but I will use it for a different purpose here. Say there were no sentient beings on earth – as will be the case someday – whatever beauty you've created will have no value at that point. I agree that the significance of the statue doesn't just reside in the clump of clay, but it does reside in the eye of the beholder.

JASON WERBELOFF

Do you feel that way about all values, not just beauty? Are things only valuable insofar as they are perceived or thought about by a specific mind? Or could they have value outside of the minds that perceive it?

DAVID BENATAR

We need to clarify what you've just said. One thing you might mean is that somebody perceives something to be valuable. The other is that there must be some perceiver in order for something to be valuable. The latter is the more charitable interpretation, because I think people certainly can be mistaken about whether something is valuable or not. Take paracetamol, a simple painkiller, which has value because of its ability to take away some relatively modest pain. You might not even appreciate it, if the paracetamol is slipped to you without your being aware, but it really relieves your pain. So that's good. That's a positive value, even if you're not aware of it. But if there's nobody to feel – no sentient beings – paracetamol ceases to have value.

JASON WERBELOFF

That makes sense because paracetamol has a certain function – to alleviate pain. If no-one's in pain – if there is a universe with no one in pain or no beings to feel pain – then its function would never be served. So, it could have no value. But it seems to me that there are other things that have value beyond their function. The value of a piece of art is not simply functional. It seems to have be something more than that.

DAVID BENATAR

A functional interpretation could be applied to art. It might be different from the one for paracetamol. Art might have an aesthetic benefit for people. For example, the posters you have on your wall presumably have some value to you as the perceiver. But if all sentient beings were obliterated, and those posters were left hanging on the wall, it's not clear to me they would have any value.

MARK OPPENHEIMER

You have suggested that from the widest possible perspective, the universal view, human lives possess an insignificant amount of value, given the vastness of time and space. But, of course, the universe is not a perceiver. It would be a mistake to look for the universe's perspective because it cannot have such a perspective.

DAVID BENATAR

You're quite correct that the universe itself doesn't have that perspective. But imagine a populated universe, with other sentient beings. In the same way that the life work of some people has significance for their fellow terrestrials, we can imagine a scenario where it has significance for people in distant corners of the universe. You might then say that from some cosmic perspective those lives have meaning.

MARK OPPENHEIMER

An implication would be that if humanity dies out but leaves a record of all of the things it has created, some other sentience (space aliens) could discover this. It may be the case that what we produced is valuable to them. They could spread it around the universe, to the delight, amusement and enlightenment of other sentient beings. That would make our lives more meaningful from the perspective of the universe, even after we've died out, wouldn't it?

DAVID BENATAR

Yes, of course, depending on the nature of that impact. Robert Nozick imagines a scenario where the purpose of our lives is to be food for intergalactic travellers. The reason why you were created was in order for the intergalactic travellers to eat you. That's some sort of cosmic purpose. But it doesn't seem to be the right sort. It's not a satisfying purpose and doesn't seem to give you the kind of answer you're looking for when you are wondering what it's all about. You don't feel it makes all the pain and striving worthwhile. So, I would want to know more about what it is that we've left behind and what it's doing for these aliens. But if it were the right sort of thing, then yes, it could posthumously, give our lives some more meaning.

JASON WERBELOFF

This reminds me about a science fiction novel which observes that we started broadcasting radio waves in the 1900s. Our TV programmes and music stations have been going out into space and reaching neighbouring star systems. The thesis of the novel is that we provide the entertainment for the galaxy, totally unbeknownst to us. One day when our programming changes, our alien neighbours get quite upset. Assuming that entertainment is meaningful, would you say that our entertainment has galactic meaning and, beyond that, eventually, universal meaning? Are you saying that our radio and TV programmes would need to impact right through the universe to have meaning?

But if we imagine that humans are the only beings, why would we think that all those distant, far-flung, unpopulated corners of the universe matter more than this particular location in determining the meaning of our lives?

DAVID BENATAR

Sometimes people phrase the concern you've raised by asking what would count as cosmic meaning? You're suggesting that if there is no life beyond earth, we can't have meaning from that broader perspective and that therefore we should not worry about it. But I can tell you what it would take for our lives to have cosmic meaning. Part of what it would take is for there to be an extra-terrestrial population and for our lives to have significance from their perspective.

But even if we set this aside it's not clear to me why we should draw comfort from your argument. Let's get back to Sisyphus again. Let's imagine that he's rolling the rock up the hill, and it keeps rolling down. He feels that it's utterly pointless. People who are watching him agree it's pointless, and he's saying 'what's my life all about?' Someone then asks Sisyphus what he would want the rolling of the rock to do in order for it to be meaningful? What meaning could come from this endless rolling of the rock? And Sisyphus is unable to answer that question. He is unable to say what could be meaningful about it. That is no source of comfort. He shouldn't at that point say that because he is unable to imagine any meaning to the process, it no longer needs to be a source of worry. His rock rolling remains futile.

JASON WERBELOFF

I wonder whether there is not a distinction between Sisyphus and the lives of most people. In the original Sisyphean case – without Taylor's modification – Sisyphus does not think his life is meaningful. He doesn't subjectively perceive his life to be meaningful. By contrast many of us do – correctly or incorrectly – think our lives are meaningful. Isn't this an important distinction?

DAVID BENATAR

Well, that's really just the difference between Sisyphus with and without the desire to roll rocks.

MARK OPPENHEIMER

One of the issues seems to be that when we're judging the significance of our lives, we don't just do so in some abstract sense, we do it comparatively. If you want to ask whether you're leading a significant life, you would look at your immediate friends and perhaps think, 'well, I'm doing okay in comparison to them'. But if we zoom out and look at the wider community, we might find our impact is rather insignificant compared to the high-profile figures. Stepping further out, comparing our significance to the Greats of Humanity – those who have saved thousands of lives or created beautiful works of art – we are likely to find our sense of the scale of our contribution to be further diminished. From the perspective of the universe, we are even less significant. But if there is no intelligent life beyond Earth – if there is just a great void – then we could limit ourselves to a kind of earthly scale of comparison which would increase our relative meaning.

DAVID BENATAR

There's a lot to be said for that view. The essential question is how should we respond to our condition? How should we respond to the fact that we can get terrestrial meaning of some kind but that other kinds of terrestrial, along with cosmic meaning, are simply not open to us? One response is to be perpetually demoralised about this. Some people might go so far as to take their own lives because they think there's no cosmic purpose. I don't think that's the right response. I don't think we should abandon the quest to make our lives more meaningful than they are. But at the same time, we shouldn't delude ourselves into thinking that they are and can be more meaningful than they actually are or can be. We should have a clear-eyed view of just how much meaning life can have. Another thing I want to say is that meaning is not about accolades or being acknowledged. Sometimes one can be identified as the person who did what one did, but that needn't always be the case. There are lots of people who do lots of good things that impact a large group of people, even though their identity is never known. I don't think that diminishes the meaning of that person's life.

MARK OPPENHEIMER

If we are trapped in a situation where our lives are less meaningful than we would like them to be and there are all these other kinds of ills that accompany existence – daily pains, the horror of death, immense suffering – what are we to do, given our human predicament?

DAVID BENATAR

The answer is not to make more humans. Once you believe this whole thing is ultimately pointless, it is ridiculous to generate more adversity-facing meaning-seekers. What about each of us who already exist? What should we do? I would suggest each of us should lead as good a life as we can – and not just morally. It is partly about improving the quality of one's own life. It is also partly about having a positive effect on those around us, either very proximately or more distantly. The net effect will be to improve one's life both in terms of its quality and its meaning.

JASON WERBELOFF

In response someone could argue that you've convinced them that there's no meaning in life – or at least that our capacity for obtaining meaning in life is much lower than we initially thought – but that there are other values in life, which are worth pursuing. So, they would agree that there's no, or very limited meaning in life but would still want to pursue a life which tries to achieve beauty or explores conceptual ideas, or whatever it is. The question is, does the 'life is meaningless' thesis extend to other values as well? Even if it is, in practice, only feasible to achieve these other ends in a very limited way?

David Benatar

Oh, indeed, I've got pessimistic views about that, too. Take knowledge, for example. There is a spectrum ranging from knowing nothing to knowing everything. As individuals, we all fall much closer to the 'know nothing' than the 'know everything' end of the spectrum. Think of all the languages that you can't speak fluently, all the knowledge in other disciplines that you don't know much about, all the things in your own discipline that you don't know. The truth is that each of us knows very, very little.

Jason Werbeloff

I can imagine two ways of one assessing that claim that we know very little. One is to think about all the possible propositions that are true. We know very few of those propositions so from that perspective the claim that we know very little is obviously correct. But perhaps there's a second sense sense in which we do know quite a lot. If we zoom out from the individual to humanity as a whole, there is a combined perspective which covers a lot of truths. Humanity is working very hard towards coming up with a theory of everything.

This would be some kind of scientific theory, trying to understand how all matter derives from an initial state, plus a set of laws, which explains how the original state brought about the next. Then we go back all the way to the initial state – the Big Bang – and then explain things going forward. That's how we could come up with some sort of theory of everything.

DAVID BENATAR

We are unduly infatuated with our own capacities. I worry about how much vicarious pride is taken by humans in what other humans are doing. There are some genius scientists discovering all these wonderful things, and we are taking some pride in that fact. But it's misplaced. We, as individuals, cannot claim any credit for their accomplishments. The other thing to notice, of course, is that a lot of those people, brilliant as they are in their in their area, have all kinds of other deficiencies. There are great minds that can probe the ends of the universe, but can't get into the mind of the person sitting next to them. In any case, it is not merely a matter of knowing propositions. Think about the sort of deeper understanding that we refer to as 'wisdom'. Some people have more of it, and some people have less of it. But any one of us has very little in comparison with what we could have in principle.

I think we should focus more on the individual for now, rather than on the collective species, because the question of meaning is a matter of the individual predicament.

MARK OPPENHEIMER

It's like standing at the base of an incredibly tall cliff, one which is probably insurmountable. We can either say we should try, in our one life, to climb the cliff as far as we can get to try and maximise the meaningful experience we can get out of life, or, when faced with the enormity of the challenge, consider it to be a worthless endeavour. I cannot undo my having been born. However, I can make a choice about whether I want to continue. So, the question, in practice is why shouldn't we kill ourselves?

DAVID BENATAR

I think there are lots of reasons not to kill yourself, not all of which have to do with the meaning of life. Those that do, involve the idea that your life can have some meaning. If meaning is a good thing, it is better having more rather than less. If you take your own life, generally speaking, you're going to be diminishing your chances for creating meaning. I'm not saying that's always the case because sometimes people achieve more meaning through their deaths than through their lives. But that's not true of the typical suicide. It is true, sometimes, of people who sacrifice their own life for some further good for others. Sometimes we can create more meaning through our own deaths. But in general, that's not the case. In general, the longer you live, all things being equal, the more meaning you can generate.

The power of the cliff analogy depends on how into cliff-climbing you are. You might just not like climbing cliffs and think you're going to stay down here at the bottom and do lots of constructive things without any climbing.

But there are other good reasons not to take your own life. One is that I think we do have an interest in continuing to exist. Those to whom we matter also have an interest in our continuing to exist. And, of course, meaning isn't everything. There are other things as well, like pleasure. Imagine that you didn't have meaning, but you could get more pleasure or other goods in life. It may be worth pursuing those, even if meaning or more meaning were beyond your reach.

You would be ill-advised to take your own life simply because you think your life doesn't have cosmic meaning.

JASON WERBELOFF

But I wonder then if you're stuck in a dilemma here? If these other things are enough to validate our lives – or at least good enough reasons not to end them – then it seems they should be enough, full stop. They should be enough to give our lives meaning. But if you if argue the pursuit of pleasure is not enough to give life meaning, well that's limited, pitiful in fact. In the scheme of things, it seems meaningless.

DAVID BENATAR

I don't see that dilemma at all. If you take meaning to be good, or at least, if there are good forms of meaning that are worth pursuing, then it would be better to have more of it, rather than less of it. And the fact that you can only have a little bit of it doesn't mean to say you shouldn't get the little bit that you can get and try to maximise how much you can get.

MARK OPPENHEIMER

Let's say that you are in an objectively awful state of

affairs, locked up in a concentration camp. You are beaten every day and deprived of almost all of life's pleasures. It is objectively an awful state of affairs. But every day you get doled out some small pleasure. A single drop of honey gets put onto your tongue or one person offers you a few kind words. Do you say, 'well, I guess this is better than nothing therefore I should persist'? Surely there's some point where we would think that those little bits of consolation don't make the whole thing worthwhile? Maybe that's what our lives really are like when we zoom out, so awful that these little bits of pleasure (or meaning) don't make continuing them worthwhile?

JASON WERBELOFF

What's so interesting about Mark's point is that so far, we've discussed the limitations on what is good. Meaning is one such good, even if its realization is limited in our lives. Mark has raised this other question, which is how much bad is there in our lives? Is Mark's objection a valid objection?

DAVID BENATAR

Mark's scenario has lumped together questions about meaning and questions about quality of life. There is of course a relationship between the two. A perception of meaning is going to enhance the quality of life. Some people might want to have a notion of quality that is so expansive that it also includes objective meaning even if the subjective assessment of that objective meaning is not present. Other people want to draw a sharp divide between the quality of life on the one hand and the meaning of life on the other. Thus, the first thing I want to do is to note that there are at least two things going on there, even if they're overlapping. The second thing is to say that I don't think that suicide is *never* the rational thing to do. If we focus only on the quality of life, we have to concede that it could be so bad that it is not in a person's interest to continue living. It may be that under certain of those circumstances, although the quality of life has fallen below zero level, there is enough meaning to justify staying alive. Thus, maybe meaning can contribute something and push a person above the zero level. But certainly, if you want to lump those two things together – meaning and quality – I think that some lives may be so bad that it is more rational to end them. What I am denying, however, is that this is generally true. No-one reading this discussion should go out and say, well, the implication is that everybody should end their own lives. Imagine that you're in an advanced stage of a terminal disease and are suffering unbearably and can only alleviate the pain by ending life. In that condition, you cannot generate any more meaning and thus it's reasonable to consider ending it all. But for you or Mark or for me, at this very moment, I don't think it's rational for us to take our lives, given the things we would be deprived of, the fact that we would be annihilating ourselves, the fact that we would be limiting the amount of meaning that we could generate in our lives, and the harm that we would do to other people. There are lots of reasons, in fact, for not ending it all.

JASON WERBELOFF

I'm curious, when you talk about annihilating yourself, whether that is bad in and of itself? Do you think that ceasing to exist is a bad thing beyond just the fact that you can no longer get good things?

DAVID BENATAR

I do think that, and I know it's not uncontroversial. I know that there are people with alternative views. My sense is that most people accept this idea implicitly. They yearn to continue existing, admittedly in part because of the goods that they can have. But very many people, under terminal conditions, who don't have much to look forward to, want to hang on to life. This tells us something about human nature, and probably about sentient nature more generally. Some might argue that this is just an irrational life drive and in fact we don't have an interest in continued existence. I don't know how to settle that question – I certainly haven't thought of a definitive answer. That's exactly why there is a dilemma once you already exist. That dilemma can be avoided by not creating new beings that will face that predicament and suffer that dilemma. And that's why I think these thoughts, again, lead to anti-natalist conclusions.

Mark Oppenheimer

Is there some sense in which you think that it's impossible to be annihilated? There's a theory of time, where the past continues to exist. You are always indelibly marked in a space-time block of the universe as existing, for all eternity, or at least until the universe itself ceases to exist. I wonder whether that sort of idea plays any role in our evaluation of our lives? If we think that in some sense we are eternal and cannot be totally annihilated.

DAVID BENATAR

I'll tell that to you when you're facing execution and see how comforted you are by it! I don't think that these sorts of weird metaphysical views are going to comfort people. But if one probes the idea in more depth. It may just be that what you mean by 'annihilated' is perfectly compatible with what I've said. It may mean that your opportunity for generating further meaning has ended. I know that this now moves into a deprivation account, but the point you make isn't limited to just the annihilation point. It would apply to deprivation as well.

MARK OPPENHEIMER

You're arguing that there are two things that are bad about dying. One is that you miss out on future goods. The other one is that the annihilation in and of itself is bad. People do seem to derive some comfort from knowing that their works will live on beyond them and that they will be remembered by their children. They might very well feel some comfort in thinking that they cannot be scrubbed from reality. Maybe my children will eventually die, I will eventually be forgotten, my work will be destroyed but in some more fundamental sense, I'm indelibly marked in the universe.

DAVID BENATAR

That's exactly how we get to this yearning for meaning. Some philosophers have suggested that the yearning comes from our own limitations. Meaning is about our transcending those limits. Some of those limitations are contained within our own lives. You reach beyond yourself when you have an impact on other people around you. Sometimes the limitations are questions about one's mortality. So, you want to reach beyond the grave, and defy death. You know it will all come to an end at some point, but at least you will survive, in some way, beyond death. That motivates a large number of people, perhaps the vast mass of humanity.

MARK OPPENHEIMER

Would our lives be better if we never died? If we were immortal would our lives be more meaningful?

DAVID BENATAR

Some philosophers, like Bernard Williams, have argued that immortality would be terrible. By definition, it goes on forever and ever. Such an existence would become infinitely boring, he says. Other philosophers have retorted that immortality needn't be boring if you have enough different kinds of pleasures and activities to engage in. You could engage in some and then move on to others and come back to some of the earlier ones later. You would gain joy and pleasure from the activity just as you do in a mortal life. So, there's a debate about that.

Immortality can't be good in an unqualified way. If you were suffering terribly and it went on forever, that would be a lot worse than suffering terribly for a period limited by your death. The question requires certain stipulations. Consider the myth of Tithonus, who was granted eternal life and just got older and more and more decrepit. The point is that eternal youth would have been much better for him than eternal *life*. Thus, one qualification that you'd have to put in place would be that you don't lose your physical and your mental faculties. Then there's the problem of you remaining alive while those close to you die. You establish and generate new families and they die. The result would be that your eternal life would be an eternal cycle of grief and relief. You may want to stipulate that your family and your friends can remain alive as well. In that case, what about the overpopulation problem? You would have to stipulate that it's a choice between procreating and being immortal – you can't have both.

Then there's the question about what happens if you do get injured and are suffering terribly. Maybe you'd want to die and thus you would have to stipulate that opting out of immortality must be an option. If you put all the stipulations in place, then it seems to me that immortality, or at least the option of immortality, would be a good thing. But immortality, without those qualifications, could be a very bad thing.

JASON WERBELOFF

A theist listening to this conversation might try the following type of argument. Assuming a universe that's barren, my life cannot have cosmic meaning. But insert God into the equation so that the broader perspective is God's perspective. Add the idea that God cares deeply about my individual life and can appreciate the value and meaning of my life from my perspective. So, we've reduced the universal perspective down to the individual perspective. Doesn't my life now have meaning?

DAVID BENATAR

I think that's exactly one of the reasons why the idea of God is so attractive. Now, I should say that, not everybody thinks that. Some atheists would argue that

God cannot give us the requisite sort of purpose, because if you were created by God to fulfil God's purposes, then you're just a pawn in God's game and have to do what God wants. They argue that if there is no God, then we are our own agents and can make our own choices. They suggest that this is more emboldening and affirming. But I do think that there's an attraction in the idea of a benevolent God – the ultimate cosmic being – bringing the right sort of meaning into our lives. The question is what the content of that meaning would be. I'm not sure how we answer that question. A common theistic move is to marvel at the mysterious ways in which God works, without filling in the details. But I do think that there would be something comforting in that idea, which is why I think it is so attractive. I just don't think it's true.

JASON WERBELOFF

To get back to the issue of whether there is some kind of life that you would want to be born into, wouldn't that life be where God does exist, and does take your life very seriously, from your point of view, and you really love your life. You really enjoy your life and believe that it's very meaningful, even if you spend your time counting your hairs or watching reruns of

Buffy the Vampire Slayer, so long as you believe very firmly that what you're doing is important. If you anchor this in God – because God believes whatever you believe – then, voila, haven't we generated a meaningful life that you would want to be born into?

DAVID BENATAR

No. That could be a version of the idyllic life, and I think that we should be indifferent between that and never existing. But remember, there is a lot in the theistic view, that has been left unsaid. We've got this kind of vague, hand-waving suggestion about how God would provide you with the requisite form of meaning. But the details are not filled out. And it's in the nature of the narrative that you can't fill them out because you're a mere mortal, whereas God could. Thus, much depends on the plausibility of accepting the idea that God does exist.

JASON WERBELOFF

Much of your work over the years has been on the topic of anti-natalism – that it is better to not have ever been. You've implied a few times during this discussion that if you could choose between the idyllic life and not to have been, you wouldn't prefer one over the other.

Why is this?

DAVID BENATAR

Because I don't think there's a net advantage to the idyllic life. It's great, if you exist, to have an idyllic life, but if you hadn't existed, you wouldn't have been deprived of it. We, as beings that exist, are deprived of everything short of the ideal. But if we'd never existed, it would not have been a loss to us. We wouldn't have been there for it to be a loss to us.

MARK OPPENHEIMER

This could be cashed out in two ways. The one is there's a non-existent entity which of course cannot, by definition, miss out on things. It cannot have Fear of Missing Out (FOMO). As it's had no prior existence, it cannot be deprived of anything. It's a state of neutralness. The other possibility is to say that never being means missing out on all the awful things that can happen in life. And that is positively good. Being committed to confronting reality for what it is means being able to recognize both the dark awful things and all of the wonderful things.

Is there some virtue in being deluded? A lot of people

will say that they're not really sure if there's a God but they're going to act as if there is one because it makes them feel happier. You've written about how people are Pollyanna-ish; they tend to look on the bright side of life. This actually makes their lives feel better even if it is a false perception. So, should we embrace a delusion? Or should we be striving for as accurate as possible a perception of reality?

DAVID BENATAR

This is a question that I discuss in my book, *The Human Predicament*. I do recognise that there can be these feedback loops. If you think that your life is better than it is, it actually becomes a bit better than it otherwise would have been, even if it doesn't become as good as you think it is. Moreover, it is true that some deviations from reality can make you feel better. But if you deviate too much, that might not actually be good for you. It's very hard to find the sweet spot. And, of course, it's also not just about you. If there are things that you can do that make your life go better, then in principle I'm in favour of them. But you need to be careful that you're not going to make things worse for other people. For example, ideologues who are so committed to a particular worldview, whether religious or secular, are likely to inflict misery on people who disagree with them. They might derive immense satisfaction from their self-righteousness, while at the same time inflicting considerable misery on other people. To come back to anti-natalist themes, I would say that if you are sufficiently deluded that you bring new beings into existence, you're doing a lot of harm in the process. Instead of opting for delusions, I would say that one should seek coping mechanisms of another kind. These include things like not focusing on suffering all the time. If you decide to focus continuously on the meaninglessness of life, this is going to become a self-fulfilling prophecy. It's a very good way to ensure you get less meaning in your life. If, instead, you could say, 'look, I'm mindful of the big picture, which is not a pretty one, but there are some things that I can do to generate some meaning in my life'. I think that would be the wiser course.

Meaning in Life through the Good, the True, and the Beautiful: Thaddeus Metz

THADDEUS METZ

Let us suppose that we have an individual who has close friendships, good collegial relationships, a loving spouse, and close ties with his children, maybe even his grandchildren. This person does charity work and has advanced social justice in some way, perhaps by winning a major court case that assisted a less-privileged community. He goes out of his way to help others by making podcasts to teach them a useful skill, like how to play chess. Furthermore, we can imagine that this person is highly educated and has obtained a few postgraduate degrees. This man also reads a lot and has come to understand much about human nature and the human environment. He might even have made discoveries in his field and published a book about these discoveries. He does not know merely about others or his world, but also knows about himself. We can imagine him to be a reflective individual, who might have spent time going through psychotherapy and thereby to have come to understand himself. He has overcome his blind spots, understands his motivations, and accepts his desires instead of pretending they do not exist. This individual is good at knowing other particular individuals, too. He can empathise with others and see the world from other people's points of view. Still more, suppose this individual has a home filled with beautiful artefacts. He attends concerts and visits museums. Perhaps in retirement, he is creative by writing poems or a novel or making sculptures. Maybe he tends a garden.

This would be a rich life. In fact, it would be an unusually rich life that few would approximate. This person's life is meaningful by virtue of exemplifying a cluster of values, which are connected with the good, the true, and the beautiful—or roughly morality, enquiry, and creativity.

We have an ideal to strive for that not many of us can likely reach. We can, however, manifest something of it. Many of us can realise a number of these kinds of values in our lives. To that extent, I suggest that many of us do have meaningful lives or lives that are meaningful on balance.

The purpose of this thought experiment is to suggest that the everyday life of a human person can exemplify meaning. The next task is to make some sense of this intuition.

One thing that is going on when English-speaking philosophers talk about what makes life meaningful is considering what conditions of a life would merit esteem or pride for oneself, and also merit admiration from the perspective of someone else. We generally think of meaning as purposes that are higher than our base desires, something greater than ourselves. We imagine ways in which we can have an interesting or compelling life story. I do not think, however, that meaning is reducible to any one of these ideas. My perspective is that when we think about meaning in life we have a cluster of different, overlapping topics in mind. The earlier example I gave of this rich life exemplifies these things. There are many conditions where it would make sense for the person to feel pride or other people to admire that individual. There are many conditions in which the individual is achieving goals that are somehow higher than his own happiness.

I gave you lots of conditions – I specified several variables, ways in which this individual could exemplify meaning in his life. One thing I seek to do as a philosopher, and many of my colleagues in the field too, is to try to unify these various ways of exemplifying meaning. We try to reduce these variables to a single property. It would be intellectually fascinating if we could come up with what we philosophers tend to call a 'theory of meaning in life' that will reduce all those properties to just one, which would be intellectually satisfying for many of us.

There are some prominent candidates in the field that I would want to criticise as candidate theories. One prominent suggestion is that life is meaningful just in so far as it fulfils God's purpose. Maybe you think that God wants you to live that kind of life that I described at the start, but I do not think that is true. Even if we suppose for the sake of argument that there is no God, we would still find a life that exemplified those conditions meaningful.

Relatedly, many are going to be much more confident that life is meaningful than they are that God exists. Put differently, you are highly justified in thinking that there is something like 'a meaningful life'. In terms of philosophy or evidence, you are much less justified in thinking God exists; in fact, you do not know that. When you encounter that kind of discrepancy in the epistemic status for your beliefs, it then becomes incoherent to maintain that a life has meaning just in so far as if it fulfils God's purpose.

A second prominent theory of life's meaning is consequentialism. You might say that tending a garden, making discoveries, or having close relationships have good consequences for yourself and other people. However, in some ways the same kind of objection as we had to the first prominent theory applies. I think we are more confident that life is meaningful than we are that that life is going to have good consequences in the long run. Indeed, we could imagine, hypothetically, that a life unexpectedly had very bad consequences for the rest of the world, and then the meaningfulness would go down to some degree. I would nevertheless want to maintain that there was some meaning by virtue of some non-consequential elements. Something in itself about that life I described at the start is important.

MARK OPPENHEIMER

There is a difference between a pleasurable life and a meaningful life, but is it possible to lead a meaningful life even if you experience personal suffering? We can imagine a Mother Teresa type figure who leads a life of abject misery while looking after people that are in states of distress and disease. Is her life meaningful?

THADDEUS METZ

My answer to your question is yes. Let's imagine the hypothetical Mother Teresa since we do not want to talk about the actual one, who seemed to have various criticisms made of her life. The hypothetical Mother Teresa, who goes out of her way to make sacrifices for others in a medical context, could be said to have meaning in her life for doing so. It would arguably be somewhat *less* meaningful if she would just be cheery when emptying the bedpans and tending to the lepers.

There would be something wrong if she was not sympathising with them in their plights and actually feeling bad. It seems, therefore, that meaning can come from unpleasant sacrifice.

We must distinguish between meaning and pleasure. A good example of this is Woody Allen's example of an orgasmatron from the movie *Sleeper*. You enter the orgasmatron, and it does what it says it is going to do. If you spent the rest of your life in the orgasmatron, then it would be a very pleasant life. It might even be a happy life. But it would not be a meaningful life. And so this thought experiment is a vivid way of seeing the difference between meaning and pleasure.

I naturally want a life with both meaning and happiness: that is probably the best life. But you are likely going to have to make some trade-offs from time to time. I would not want to live the hypothetical Mother Teresa life for the rest of my life. But my way of understanding that is to say that meaning is not everything. Happiness counts too. It is just a different value.

JASON WERBELOFF

To summarise what you have said, we are investigating a particular value and that is meaning. We are trying to find an account of meaning. What meaning boils down to. And your account sounds like it is a combination of three factors: the good, the beautiful and the true. You also looked at competing accounts, such as the religious one. In the religious account, meaning boils down to God or following God's word. You stated that the religious account is not going to work. You have also examined consequentialism, where meaning is wrapped up in actions that produce good consequences, and you said that is not going to work either because of these counterexamples.

Now, I am just curious why you have chosen those three factors, the good, the beautiful, and the true. Are they all necessary? Are they together sufficient for me to have meaning in life?

THADDEUS METZ

I focus on those three because they are common ground in analytical philosophical debates over the past 100 years. If you go back to the turn of the 20th century, around the 1900s or late 19th century even, when you start getting English-speaking philosophers theorising about meaning and you work your way up until the present day, you will find that the overwhelming majority of them accept that the good, the true, and the beautiful are relatively uncontroversial instances of meaning. Each element contributes to a life's meaning. And this is the case for religious folks, consequentialists, and broadly deontologists like me. What might those three conditions have in common? Can we reduce them to something? The religious theorist says it is God's purposes. The consequentialist says it is consequences. My view roughly is that it is a kind of exercise of rational nature. I take a broadly Aristotelian or Kantian perspective on what unifies those three conditions and explains why each makes a life more meaningful. So that is the dialectic.

JASON WERBELOFF

I have got an alternative for you, Thad. I am a perfectionist, so I particularly like perfection as a value. When you describe this life, this person who teaches others chess, this person who reads and self reflects and go to psychoanalysis and learns various skills, gardens, I wonder whether you are not describing lots of different types of perfection. A perfection roughly means a skill or an art, something that one becomes good at. One does not have to be perfectly good at it, but it seems like that person is living a perfect life in some sense, rather than a meaningful life. Would that not describe their lives?

THADDEUS METZ

I do not think that would be inaccurate. It depends on what we mean by 'meaning'. Why must it be perfection instead of meaning? If I define meaning of life as those conditions that merit pride or admiration or about getting in touch with something greater than yourself or constructing a compelling life story, then these properties seem to capture what is going on in this life. I could possibly describe it in other terms, such as perfection. I do not think I necessarily disagree. I just would not want to exclude the possibility of meaning capturing it.

The other thing to say is I would want to know more about what makes something a perfection. It is not enough to say that these are skills, or perfections, because we want to know in virtue of what are they perfections. One way to understand my project is to try to give you an account of what makes something a perfection. Again, you could in your terms see the religious view and the consequentialist view and the deontological view as rival accounts of the same cluster of stuff.

MARK OPPENHEIMER

You alluded earlier to this idea of a compelling life story and how that might make your life meaningful. We can think about tyrants and fascist leaders or communist leaders as having incredibly compelling life stories and having this gigantic impact on their nation and their world at large but that impact is pernicious. They act with evil. You might think that they have a particular end in mind and that they use their rational faculties to get that end, and that they were happy with that end. Hitler aimed to exterminate all Jews. When some survived he might say that there was a failing, but he was nevertheless engaged in this project through a rational process. In other words, the goal he wanted and the means he used to get there was rational. Now we all accept it is an entirely evil process, but it is one with a big impact and it is a compelling life story in the sense that it is a story that will be remembered for many years to come. Is Hitler's life meaningful?

THADDEUS METZ

There are lots of things to say about the case. There are two things I will focus on. The first thing is I distinguish, as Robert Nozick does in his work, between a meaningful life and an impactful life. Nozick thinks there is a difference between saying a life is significant on the one hand and a life has been impactful on another, and I agree. From here, we can debate the value of an impactful life but I would suggest that on the face of it, it is not necessarily a meaningful life. When we talk about meaning, the overwhelming majority of philosophers have in mind something positive, something desirable. Therefore, merely having an impact, destroying the earth, for example, is not a good candidate.

The second thing to say is that what I try to do in some of my work is to say more about the nature of that rationality. So if I were to cash out Jason's perfections I would go running to Aristotle and Kant roughly and say an awful lot of perfection is a function of the exercise of intelligence of some kind. But rationality has to be exercised in a particular way. And Hitler did not do it right. The right exercise of rationality is when it is positively oriented towards fundamental aspects of human life. For example, what makes love meaningful, according to me, is that it involves intelligence. Animals cannot love, at least not in the way that we find particularly meaningful. Love involves emotional intelligence, quite literally, where what we prize about the other person and what we respond to positively is her character. When we love somebody in a meaningful way we appreciate what makes her tick and we support that. It is not just the fact she has moles or freckles. It is not just her appearance. We might like her appearance and it might give us pleasure, but it is not a meaningful connection. Rather, it is her character that makes her tick, what is responsible for much else about her life. When we love it, that is the source of a meaningful connection.

Another example of fundamentality is Einstein and Darwin's discoveries. What makes them so terrifically important is that space and time explain much else about the nature of the universe, and evolution is responsible for an awful lot about the course of human existence. What I try to do in my book *Meaning in Life* is show how fundamentality is at the root of much of our thinking about substantial meaning in life. Returning to Hitler, I would say he was not positively orienting his intelligence towards humans, or what is fundamental to humans. He was negative, in the sense of killing, destroying.

JASON WERBELOFF

What is interesting is this distinction that Mark asked you to draw between meaning and impact, is that the impact of a life is not significant enough to generate meaning from it. However, there is another distinction about which I am curious. You have partly answered it, but it is a distinction a lot of people do not make and that is the difference between a meaningful life and a purposeful life. People often use those terms interchangeably and I wonder whether that is correct.

THADDEUS METZ

Part of what we have in mind when we are thinking about meaning is purpose. But it has got to be a particular kind of purpose. It cannot be just any purpose. Otherwise, we wind up with a kind of subjectivist account, where it could be a higher-order purpose to become the world's long-distance spitting champion. It might be worth doing but I would not want to say that it is meaningful or important. So there are certain kinds of purpose that we have in mind when talking about meaning.

I do not think that every sort of meaning in life is a matter of involving some kind of purpose or activity. There can be certain kinds of passive conditions, such as being loved. If you are loved, your life has probably got some amount of meaning by virtue of that, without you really doing anything necessarily. Your life would be all the more meaningful if you loved back and fulfilled a purpose. But simply being the object of somebody's care, concern, and affection probably makes your life somewhat more important, and that does not seem to me to involve any purposeful activity of much worth.

JASON WERBELOFF

You are saying purpose is neither necessary nor sufficient for meaning, because you can imagine cases where it is missing and you still have meaning, and cases where it is present and you still do not have meaning. There was a term you used there that I think it is really interesting in this discussion. That is subjectivism. So there are these interesting distinctions between subjectivism and objectivism about meaning. Is meaning the kind of thing that it is determined by you, the person who holds the meaning, or is meaning something objective that can describe the way you live your life independently of whether you believe it is meaningful or not?

THADDEUS METZ

That is a classic distinction in the field. For much of the 20th century, the subjectivists had held the upper hand. However, over the past 20/30 years, the objectivists have come to the fore. These days a very large majority of philosophers believe you can be mistaken about what makes your life meaningful or not. You might find something meaningful or something might be meaningful to you, but that does not necessarily mean that it is actually meaningful or makes it worth choosing or is actually something that merits pride or admiration on the part of others. I think the long-distance spitting case seems probably as good an example as any.

MARK OPPENHEIMER

In your book, you have a wonderful page of examples of this. You ask how a person derives meaning from standing in queues for hours on end. Or from maintaining a precise number of hairs on their head?

Or eating their own faeces? Or re-watching episodes of Buffy the Vampire Slayer? These are all knockdown objections to this notion that meaning could be purely subjective. In other words, it may be the kind of thing you find very pleasurable and you feel like it is meaningful but that does not make it so.

THADDEUS METZ

One thing the subjectivist has right is that our lives would be more meaningful if we were subjectively attracted to these objectively worthwhile conditions. If we are doing the right sort of thing, and we believe it to be the right sort of thing, and we actually like it, all the better normally (but the Mother Teresa case above might be an exception) .

MARK OPPENHEIMER

It seems that you have to strive for the right goal and there is an alignment between your internal mental states and the right object. There is a subjective role to be played in this exercise, but it's just not the sole determinant of meaning.

THADDEUS METZ

I think that is probably the dominant view these days, although this view has its variations. In my variant, you do not need to have any subjective elements at all to have meaning in life. We can go back to the hypothetical Mother Teresa from earlier on and suppose she really hates what she is doing. She does not believe it is important, but so long as she is actually saving lives and relieving pain, in my view there is some meaning there, even if there is room for more. But the more common view is Susan Wolf's, where she believes that subjective attraction is a necessary condition for having meaning.

MARK OPPENHEIMER

There are different ways you could cash subjective attraction out. The one might be that it is an amplifier and the one is that it is necessary. So if you imagine that the Mother Theresa who feels nothing or feels total negativity about the exercise, her apathy either diminishes it or means that the activity is entirely meaningless. I like the idea of being able to have an almost mathematical formula for working out what activity you would engage in be meaningful. One part of the equation is what the activity is and part of it is it your view on the activity.

The issue I would like to return to is this notion of impact. We discussed Professor David Benatar, who has written about an aligned topic, which is what is the meaning of life. He says it might very well be the case that you can experience meaningful things in the terrestrial realm. You can engage in these beautiful and true and good things. But ultimately when we zoom out, when we look at things from the perspective of the universe, the impact of our lives is so tiny, so minuscule, that it is irrelevant. Therefore, overall our lives are rather meaningless.

THADDEUS METZ

You can take that perspective, but it is hard for me to see why we should. There are a number of concerns I have about this kind of perspective. Most obviously, the first concern is that there are mighty high standards that are being set up for meaning and very few of us would have similarly high standards when it comes to other values. To illustrate, you do not need to be Jesus to be aptly described as a morally good person or a virtuous person. You do not need to have been plugged into the orgasmatron for an eternity to have a life that is properly described as a happy life. You do not need to be able to break planets by snapping your fingers to be aptly described as strong. So when we look at other values, which are simply adjectives, we have much more mundane or everyday standards that we tend to invoke. It is hard for me to see why we should go reaching for a cosmic perspective when thinking about meaning in particular. I do not think it is qualitatively different from these other kinds of values.

The second thing I want to say about this argument from Professor Benatar is that I see an incoherence in it. He has awfully high standards of perfection. His ideal of perfection is not the same sense as Jason's, but a very idealised standard for meaning. His view entails that we have got to be able to make a major difference to the universe to count as having a meaningful life, or at least a cosmically meaningful life which Professor Benatar thinks is incredibly important. But he does not have similar standards when it comes to epistemology and making these kinds of judgements. So Professor Benatar thinks we should believe his view. He thinks he has good arguments for his view. So notice this normative and evaluative language there. But he is using everyday standards when he is advancing his philosophy. He is not appealing to perfection when he tells us what would be good to believe or what we should believe. By the same token let us not use perfection or such high standards when we are thinking about how we should live or what a desirable life would be. If we are going to be consistent and use everyday standards when it comes to epistemology and justification of belief, then we should use similar standards when thinking about what kind of life is justified or appropriate.

JASON WERBELOFF

David Benatar's view is not totally nihilistic. He does think there is some meaning in life. He just thinks it is vastly reduced than what we think it is. It is just this terrestrial meaning which sits in a tiny little band below cosmic meaning and he views cosmic as the important type of meaning.

But I am curious about a different nihilism. What if I were to ask you about the true, the good, and the beautiful. These things exist, but that is all there is. There is no meaning that is built upon them. Meaning is not reducible to them. Meaning is eliminated and all we are left with is those three things. What would you think about an eliminativist view of meaning?

THADDEUS METZ

We could get rid of meaning talk, but we would still have the meaningful conditions. We just would not use the word 'meaningful' to refer to them. An analogy would be that we could talk about H_2O without ever using the word 'water', but water would still exist. There would still be H_2O and what today we call 'water'. So if we have the good, the true, and the beautiful, we can avoid using 'meaning' talk to refer to them. But that stuff really is what constitutes meaning. Simply removing the language is not particularly powerful. I do not see what the motivation would be. I do not feel very threatened by it either because the actual values would still be obtained.

MARK OPPENHEIMER

It seems like you do have some underlying framework in which you have slotted these three valuable things. You spoke earlier about love. Do you see love as a free-standing value or can it be explained partly in relation to the others? That to be in love is partly to desire someone beautiful? To be in love is to maybe treat them in a good way, to have respect for them, to want good things to happen to them, and maybe also to understand them, so find it what is true about them. It would seem that love could be explained in three ways. But perhaps there is more to love. Perhaps we cannot just boil down love to these three values. Maybe there is something left over after we have done the reduction exercise.

THADDEUS METZ

That seems accurate since I think there are probably lots of reasons to value love. I am suggesting one reason to love is that it is meaningful. It makes your life more important to love and to be loved. It is something that would merit pride. Love is something that is worth doing that transcends your animal nature. But another reason to love is that it can be pleasant and bring you happiness. That is just a distinct kind of way of valuing love. I am not trying to suggest the only reason to love is that is meaningful, that love involves the kind of exercise of intelligence that I think that makes a life important. It is not the only reason, but it is one reason.

MARK OPPENHEIMER

What are we to do when we are faced with meaningful activities that are at odds with each other? For example, imagine you could find out what is actually true but it may be an ugly truth or it may be very unkind to others. Should we reveal that truth? Do you have some underlying framework which tells you how to pursue meaning when you have trade-offs to make?

THADDEUS METZ

I do not. The only people who do have such a framework are the consequentialists at this stage. In principle, the consequentialists assign a cardinal number to each value state and they think that you can you count up what the numerical outcomes of various choices would be. That is the only view that I can think of that has some kind of structure for making trade-offs. The lack of such a framework is a weak part of the field that merits development. The development of a non-consequentialist way to rank different kinds of the meaning would be well worth doing. Nobody has gotten very far yet. I have not myself.

JASON WERBELOFF

This seemingly raises a bigger problem: Can you ever know (a) how meaningful life is and (b) whether it is meaningful given that you cannot even rank these different options?

THADDEUS METZ

We can rank them, but we cannot yet rank them with precision. We cannot yet say what is behind the ranking. I am quite happy to say that the lives of Mandela and Einstein were more meaningful than mine. One played a major role in freeing an entire country from Apartheid, and the other made a major discovery about the nature of the universe. Those are big. We perhaps cannot quantify these contributions, but we can compare them to most lives and say: 'Well, that stands out.' There is a good reason why those two lives are often used as exemplars of meaningfulness. We can make confident judgments of rankings, but precision and explanation are still missing.

JASON WERBELOFF

You mentioned different types of values which might compete with meaning in any given circumstance where we might have to choose between these different types of values. One you mentioned was happiness or pleasure. Another one was perfection which might be more closely aligned with meaning. There are others as well like morality, and perhaps a sense of adventure. I wonder how you would rank meaning compared with those. Often what we are trying to get at when we ask for an account of meaning or an account of happiness, we want to know how to live our lives. So, we want an answer to the question of how to live or an instruction on how to live your life according to these factors. But, if I live a life that is good, true, and beautiful, then that will only get me meaning. Now, I also have to look at how do I live a moral life and what happens when I have sacrificed a bit of morality for a bit of meaning or vice versa. What is the balance there that I need between all these different values?

THADDEUS METZ

That is a tough question and one that no philosophers have a particularly good answer to. One thing that most philosophers would agree on, however, is that with any of these values, you do not want to go beneath a certain floor. If we are trying to be moral, we do not want to be a Hitler. When it comes to happiness, you do not want to be tortured for very long. When it comes to meaning, you do not want to be stuck in the orgasmatron for the rest of your life.

Supposing that you have got enough of each of these kinds of values, then you see what is on offer given your particular temperament, society, and environment. Supposing you have got enough morality, happiness, and meaning where now? Can you really go to town concerning the other values? Many of us would accept that broad picture of how to live.

MARK OPPENHEIMER

Early in the pandemic, you wrote a short piece about how we can have an anti-matter, the sort of thing that erodes meaning in our lives. You used the example of the endless cycle of sanitising, of having to make sure that your hands are clean, that your car is clean, that you are wearing your mask properly. We wind up in this banal cycle where nothing ever really is accomplished and you do the same thing over and over again.

Now that strikes me as a meaningless thing to do. If we engage in enough meaningless acts, then those acts start to erode the meaningful things in our lives. Are there other kinds of 'anti-matter' than can take a once meaningful life and destroy it?

THADDEUS METZ

Repetitiveness is a good example of something that might erode meaning, even if we are repeatedly doing good things. With Covid-19 at least you are repetitively doing something for a good cause. Similarly, in the movie *Groundhog Day*, you have got Bill Murray actually doing good things - rescuing people, playing the piano, giving gifts. But, something is lacking in meaning when it is literally the same activities done every 24 hours. Repetitiveness drains life of meaning.

Causing harm is another clear example of meaning in life being eroded. The Hitler example is a good one in this case. In my book, I imagine somebody who blows up the Sphinx for fun. So, when one destroys great works of art, then it is not just that meaning is absent. It is that those kinds of actions reduce the meaningfulness of your life. There is an important difference between blowing up the Sphinx just for fun and oversleeping. If you oversleep, then no meaning is added to your life, but it does not *reduce* the meaning of your life in the way that blowing up the Sphinx would.

JASON WERBELOFF

I have two questions. The first is, might your account of the meaning of life not be missing the criterion of novelty? Does novelty boil down to any of the good, the beautiful and the true? If it does not, then it seems like we need to add novelty.

The second question I have is whether activities are meaningful or life is meaningful or both?

THADDEUS METZ

In the book, I add an advancement criterion to particularly great sources of meaning. If we are talking about truth or knowledge, then making a discovery is better than just engaging with something that someone has already discovered. When we talk of great meaning in life, it is indeed related to newness or originality.

There is good debate about what the ultimate bearer of a meaningful life is. In my view, it is both actions considered in themselves, and then also the life as a whole. If somebody finds a cure for cancer after working hard on that for many years, I am inclined to say that discovery adds to the meaning of his or her life, even if I know nothing else about her life. If we agree with that judgment, then we can say that actions in themselves can bear meaning. On the other hand, there can be patterns in the way people live over time that are independent sources of meaning. Many of us want our lives to improve over time. We want our lives to develop on an upwards slope, even if our life starts a bit low. We would prefer a life that starts low and improves over a life that starts high and then deteriorates over time, even if the amount of the good, the true, and the beautiful were constant in both lives. This suggests to me that it is not only the actions that bear meaning but also the pattern of the life. The life as a whole seems to be able to be appraised as meaningful or meaningless. I think those are two independent ways of judging a life for its meaning.

MARK OPPENHEIMER

If we talk about discovering something true, we might think of it as being an objective thing in the world. Similarly, with the good – we might have an objective account of morality, and so be able to determine what the right thing to do is. The beautiful seems more complicated. Can we say that an artist is producing a beautiful work? What about an artist who creates grotesque works and is nevertheless revered?

How do we determine whether someone who is an artist is actually doing something meaningful?

THADDEUS METZ

When talking about the beautiful, we should consider something broader, like creativity. While we might consider aesthetically appealing visual arts or music, we should not limit our conception of what is meant by 'the beautiful' in this context only to that. There could be ugly arts that are nonetheless creative and revealing and that prompt us to see the world differently. That artwork would count as 'beautiful', that is, creative, aesthetically valuable, and hence meaningful for my project. The word 'beautiful' is not meant to be read narrowly. I would even include humour when I think of the beautiful. Having a sense of humour is a kind of creativity and would fall under this heading.

A further question could be how do we know what is aesthetically valuable. I would say that we ought to use our senses, listen to art critics, and consider what philosophers say. That seems to be the normal way of trying to judge a work of art or judge a work of creativity.

JASON WERBELOFF

Let's turn our attention to the true.

I wonder if there isn't a counter-example that we can use against the veneration of truth. Consider the *Toa Te Ching* where Lao Tzu talks about the importance of misinformation. He says it is important that the populace does not believe what is true, because if they do, they will rebel and there will be discord in the land. So, it is important to sew enough misinformation and lack of education into people's lives for them to have a peaceful existence. This entails that the most meaningful leader will be the one who does not promote the truth entirely.

THADDEUS METZ

By 'true' I do not literally mean propositions that correspond to the facts. The 'true' is a placeholder for enquiry or intellectual reflection. That includes merely justifiable beliefs that are false for example. It could also include certain kinds of awareness that do not involve analysis or deliberation, such as empathy or certain types of cognitive awareness ascribed to mystics. These examples are going to count as enquiry or intelligence very broadly construed. I would want to capture them as good candidates for some of the meaning in a life.

Concerning the political case of trading truth for the sake of peace, my response to that would be that a good leader might be one who sacrifices the truth for the sake of peace. But would it not be an even more impressive leader who found a way not to have to make that trade-off? Would that not be all the better if a leader could promote both goods of truth and peace? And if we want to say yes to that, then that suggests that there is something important about truth in itself.

There is the further question of how much weight truth has relative to other goods. So the claim I want to defend is that some kinds of reflection are meaningful, but not that they are all important.

MARK OPPENHEIMER

So David Benatar is famous for another view which is this notion that it is wrong to bring new life into the world because life is overall filled with more suffering than it is filled with pleasure and therefore it will be better for you not have been born. He does not only use this pleasure/pain analysis. He partly relies on his account of why life is not nearly as meaningful as we think it is.

But let us imagine that your view is correct – we don't need the cosmic view of meaning, and we can determine meaning on a more terrestrial scale, but it is true that life involves more suffering than pleasure. Could we then argue that it is not immoral to bring new life into the world on the basis that those beings have the capacity to experience meaning and that meaning might trump the suffering?

THADDEUS METZ

That is precisely the kind of move I have suggested in response to Professor Benatar's works. He does not want to restrict his analysis to pain and pleasure, but the argument works most naturally when we are looking at welfarist values like happiness and unhappiness. I do think meaning is a distinct value and it can provide good reason to procreate. If my children are going to have meaningful lives—so long as it is not the terribly self-sacrificial sort that we discussed earlier—then I think that it is a good reason to have created them.

MARK OPPENHEIMER

Do you think that to lead a meaningful life there are certain prerequisites that one has to have? Are their certain human beings who by their nature cannot lead meaningful lives and are there other kinds of non-human beings that could lead meaningful lives?

THADDEUS METZ

My account focuses on rationality and the exercise of intelligence, which entails a concern with persons as the kinds of beings that can live meaningfully or not. Not only humans but intelligent aliens could also have meaningful lives. If God exists, then God could have a meaningful life.

The question then arises about certain animals, such as pets. Can dogs and cats live meaningful lives? Since I have suggested that being loved might confer some meaning on an individual's life, there can be some limited sort of meaning in pets' lives by them being part of a loving relationship. I am not sure it counts for all that much compared to the kinds of meaning which a human person could exhibit. But it seems that the kind of life that a cat or dog could live when it is a pet is more meaningful than a spider living out in the wild. I am more readily inclined to say that the former's life has *some* kind of significance that the latter lacks.

MARK OPPENHEIMER

We might think the claim about meaning in lives only make sense relationally. If the average spider lives for 27 days and this one has lived for 60 days, then this spider has lived a long life. Similarly, one might say that this cat has a meaningful life in relation to other cats, and this human has a meaningful life in relation to other humans. However, is it not incoherent to cross the categories and to make claims about supernatural beings?

In the same vein, we can think about relationships. You have done work on African ethics, and this view suggests that there is a relationship involved in finding out what the right thing is to do. Is my capacity for meaning restricted if I live on a desert island on my own? Do we require other people to have relationships with to lead a truly meaningful life?

THADDEUS METZ

It is one place where I disagree with much of the African tradition actually. A lot of the African tradition focuses on relationality or community. Certainly, when it comes to morality, the thought is that to be a virtuous person, I have to interact positively with other persons in some way. I am inclined to think that this might be right when it comes to morality.

However, I do think the focus on relationality is wrong when it comes to meaning. I have used the thought experiment of the hypothetical Robinson Crusoe who has been shipwrecked and who is now isolated on a deserted island. Could that individual live a meaningful life? I think, yes, he can. Let's imagine two different Robinson Crusoes. The first one engages in wishful thinking. He thinks he is going to be rescued soon, but there is no evidence for that. In fact, there is lots of evidence against his imminent rescue. He gets addicted to a local plant. He is terrified of the warthogs on the island. He does not go out of his way to decorate his shelter; he just makes do with a cave. This Robinson Crusoe is not doing so well when it comes to meaning. But imagine a second Crusoe. He has accepted the fact that he is not going to be rescued and he has kicked his addiction to the plant. He has battled the warthogs courageously. He designs a beautiful shelter for himself.

The second Crusoe is clearly faring better, and it seems to be because he is living a more meaningful life than the first one. So, I do not think other persons are necessary to have meaning in life. It might be that having a life devoid of other humans can be a meaningful life but not a particularly meaningful life. I am naturally open to the idea that life is more meaningful if there are other persons. But I would not want to say that the existence of other persons is necessary for a significant existence.

JASON WERBELOFF

I think that is a particularly useful takeaway given that a lot of countries are going through a second wave of Covid and people are being forced to isolate again. I think it is consoling that one can, in principle at least, live a meaningful life alone.

POSTSCRIPT 1:
DAVID BENATAR'S RESPONSE TO THADDEUS METZ

In my *Brain In a Vat* interview on the meaning of life, I did not directly engage Thaddeus Metz's views on meaning in life. In his subsequent interview, in response to an explicit question from Mark Oppenheimer, Professor Metz offered a critique of one central feature of my view. I am taking the publication of this book as an opportunity to offer a brief reply.

Mark Oppenheimer noted that while I think that our lives can be meaningful to varying degrees from various terrestrial perspectives, our lives can have no cosmic meaning, and that the absence of cosmic meaning is unfortunate.

Thaddeus Metz's response was that while one *could* take a cosmic perspective, he said it was hard for him to see why we *should*. He offers two argument for this conclusion.

According to his first argument, taking the cosmic perspective sets up excessively high standards for meaning – standards that Professor Metz claims we would not employ when it comes to values other than meaning. He says that:

> you do not need to be Jesus to be aptly described as a morally good person or a virtuous person. You do not need to have been plugged into the orgasmatron for an eternity to have a life that is properly described as a happy life. You do not need to be able to break planets by snapping your fingers to be aptly described as strong.

It is true that when we say that somebody is good, or happy, or strong, we are making those judgements relative to their fellow humans. We are saying something like 'by human standards, this person is good, or happy, or strong'. It is entirely reasonable to make such a claim (when it is true). However, it does not follow from this that even the best, happiest, or strongest people are good, happy or strong from some broader perspective.

Strength may be the easiest case to consider by way of example. Rhinos and elephants are much stronger than the strongest humans. It is one thing to say that somebody is a strong human. It is quite another to live in denial that elephants are much stronger – and that elephants are much weaker than an omnipotent being would be.

Alternatively, imagine one were considering how well a long-tailed field mouse's life should be rated on a longevity scale. One would correctly say of a two-year old mouse of this species that, by the standards of the species, this particular mouse has lived a long time. But that is surely not the *only* standard by which we can judge the mouse's longevity. We can *also* compare the mouse's lifespan to a bowhead whale (which has a life expectancy of 200 years). From that perspective, it makes perfect sense to say that the mouse does not live very long. Moreover, it is sad that mouse lives are so short – that mice do not have much longer lifespans than they actually have. Insofar as it is better to have longer lives, mice do not fare as well as whales.

I make a similar claim about meaning. Some lives can be very meaningful by human standards. (Other human lives are much less meaningful even by human standards.) However, even the most meaningful of human lives are not very meaningful by ideal standards, and this is cause for sadness.

If I had claimed that we should examine the meaning of human lives *only* from the cosmic perspective, then I would have been liable to Professor Metz's objection. However, my view is that meaning should be assessed from all perspectives in order to determine those from which a life does and those from which a life does not have meaning. We do *that* for other values. By Professor Metz's own logic, then, we should do the same for meaning.

Does it make a difference that whereas a mouse's longevity can be compared to a whale's, the meaning of the most meaningful human lives cannot be compared with any actual lives that *do* have cosmic meaning (for the simple reason that, on my view, there are no lives that have cosmic meaning)? I don't think so. No animals live for five hundred years and yet we can say of the bowhead whale that while it is very lucky to live so much longer than other animals, it is unfortunate for not having a still longer lifespan – perhaps of five hundred years.

Professor Metz has a second argument. Here he suggests that my view is incoherent. He says that whereas I have very high standards for meaning, I do not 'have similar standards when it comes to epistemology and making ... judgements' about the meaning of lives. In the latter case, he says, I am 'using everyday standards' rather than 'appealing to perfection'.

This argument fares no better than the first. We are all epistemically limited. Some people's epistemic limitations include an inability to see that they are epistemically limited. For the rest of us, however, our epistemic limitation does not include an inability to see that limitation. If somebody who is epistemically limited were to argue that it is a great pity that we are as epistemically limited as we are, it would be absurd to respond that the argument is incoherent because it uses ordinary standards of reasoning to conclude that perfect standards of reasoning would be better. It makes no more sense to suggest that an epistemically limited argument is incoherent for reaching the conclusion that it would be better if our lives had not only terrestrial meaning but also cosmic meaning.

In other words, we can only offer the best arguments we can. It does not follow from this that the conclusions we reach may not include the claims that:

a. Our arguments are much less good than those of an infallible, perfectly rational, omniscient being would be.

b. Our lives are much less meaningful than they would be if they had both terrestrial and cosmic meaning.

Finally, I shall note, but not say much about a fleeting response that Professor Metz offers to my anti-natalist views. He says that if one's 'children are going to have meaningful lives – so long as it is not the terribly self-sacrificial sort ... –then ... that it is a good reason to have created them'.

I disagree. Once one has been brought into existence, it is indeed prudentially better if one's life has more meaning rather than less. However, it does not follow from this that we should create more meaning-seekers.

A life never started is one that can never be deprived of meaning. While we are right to worry about the meaning of actual lives, it would be a mistake to start worrying about the meaning of lives that were never begun.

POSTSCRIPT 2:
BRIEF REJOINDER FROM THADDEUS METZ TO DAVID BENATAR

In the course of my dialogue with Mark Oppenheimer and Jason Werbeloff about meaning in life, I had made two potshots at a view that David Benatar has advanced. Benatar believes not merely that our lives would be better if they were cosmically meaningful, but also, and more strongly, that our lives are 'unfortunate' and are a 'cause for sadness' since they are not cosmically meaningful. The quoted phrasings are from 'David Benatar's Response to Thaddeus

Metz', wherein Benatar responds to my two criticisms. In this short rejoinder, I indicate why I think that Benatar's responses have not settled these matters, meaning that these criticisms of the view that a cosmically meaningless life is bad merit further consideration.

The first criticism I had made is an analogy. I had pointed out that perfection is unnecessary to describe certain lives accurately as exhibiting certain goods such as moral virtue, happiness, and strength. Just as one need not be Jesus in order to count as virtuous, so one need not have an impact on the cosmos in order for one's life to count as meaningful. Benatar responds that such judgements are sensibly made from a limited, human perspective, but that it is open to us to take a broader perspective from which it would be inappropriate to make them.

On this score, Benatar draws his own analogy, pointing out that we can sensibly make judgements about strength and longevity not merely amongst members of a given species, but also between species. It is coherent to say that elephants are stronger than us and whales live longer than mice. By analogy, Benatar concludes, it is coherent to say that our lives are unfortunate and a cause for sadness for not being the sort of people who make a difference to the universe.

The issue of how to appraise lives comparatively is grossly under-developed in the field of philosophy. I lack conclusive or even firm suggestions at this point. However, what I can suggest at this stage is that there is a prima facie difference between the two cases that Benatar presents and the conclusion he would like to infer from them.

I think it is fair to say that elephants are stronger than us and that whales live longer than mice. And it might be reasonable to hold that it would be better if we were as strong as elephants and if mice lived as long as whales. However, it seems a leap to conclude that our lives are (in some respect) *bad, i.e., unfortunate and a cause for sadness*, for not being as strong as elephants or that the lives of mice are bad for not living as long as whales. Similarly, I baulk at the suggestion that we should conclude that our lives are bad for not exhibiting cosmic meaning, even if, at this stage of reflection, I am willing to grant that they would be better if they (somehow) did.

Perhaps Benatar would hold that our lives would be bad *from a cosmic standpoint*, whereas they would not be bad from a human standpoint. However, our lives would analogously be very good from a standpoint even more limited than that of humanity, say, that of the mouse. From which perspective should we appraise a human life? Benatar remarks in his 'Response' that 'meaning should be assessed from all perspectives in order to determine those from which a life does and those from which a life does not have meaning'. Now, does this mean that all perspectives are 'equally valid'? How to proceed when they ground differing appraisals? Is there any reason to think that the cosmic perspective is more authoritative than the human one? Clearly we normally work with a human perspective when judging lives as virtuous, happy, strong, or meaningful—why should we take up other perspectives?

As I continue to think about these matters, I intend to explore the hunch that the absence of a good merits being described as 'unfortunate' or a 'cause for sadness', the more available it is to us. So, when I have had a good such as a family, job, or longevity and I am then deprived of it, it is clearly described as 'unfortunate' or a 'cause for sadness'. When I have not had a good, but would have had it were it not for avoidable injustice that has taken place, then, again, it is fairly described that way. When I have not had a good such as longevity, but would have had it were it not for a lack of technological know-how that will be developed in 100 years' time, then it also might (I am less sure) be fairly described that way. However, these cases seem different from those in which there is no proximate world in which I could have the good. It appears physically impossible for humans (or even for *us*, given those who doubt that *we* are essentially *human*) to make a cosmic difference, and so I doubt that the absence of this good renders our lives bad.

I turn now to the second criticism I had made of Benatar's position that our lives are bad for failing to exhibit cosmic meaning. It was a charge of a kind of incoherence. On the one hand, Benatar judges our lives from a cosmic standpoint, finding them lacking in meaning and hence to be bad. On the other hand, when Benatar advances this very position about the quality of our lives, he does not take up a parallel cosmic standpoint in respect of the quality of reasoning. If he took up a cosmic standpoint in respect of the quality of reasoning, he would probably have to conclude that we know little and that our analysis—including his own argumentation—is poor. However, when he advances his position on life's meaninglessness, he implicitly holds that he knows enough to draw a conclusion about the quality of our lives and that his analysis is good. If he is not going to take up a cosmic perspective when evaluating his argumentation as good or bad, then, I suggested, he should not take up a cosmic perspective when evaluating a life as good or bad. Otherwise, there is an inconsistency in standards being invoked.

In his response, Benatar's core remark is: 'If somebody who is epistemically limited were to argue that it is a great pity that we are as epistemically limited as we are, it would be absurd to respond that the argument is incoherent because it uses ordinary standards of reasoning to conclude that perfect standards of reasoning would be better.'

However, I think there could well be an incoherence here, depending on what the interlocutor is imagined to hold. If someone maintains that we must use perfect standards of reasoning to evaluate an argument, and if he then does not use such standards in the course of advancing *that* argument and judges this argument to be a good one, there is a tension. It would be natural to say to this person, 'You are making an argument that you implicitly think is good, good enough for others to consider and even have them change their minds. However, you are not adhering to perfect standards of argumentation. Therefore, in the act of making this argument, you are committed to the view that imperfect standards of argumentation will suffice when judging the quality of argumentation.'

Similarly, when Benatar maintains that his argumentation about life's meaning is justified or otherwise has epistemic value, he is working with a human perspective and implicitly holding that to be sufficient when appraising knowledge claims. To reject—in the course of doing so—the human perspective as inadequate when appraising lives seems like a tension to me. It would be more consistent for him to judge his own arguments about life's meaning to be inadequate from a god-like standpoint. If he wants to maintain, though, that his argumentation is good, then we are back to a human standpoint, which in turn seems fair to use to conclude that a life is good.

These are complex matters, and, even within my

human perspective, I realize I have surely not had the last word on them. I am grateful to have had my horizons broadened by engaging with David Benatar, and I look forward to the field thinking more about these fascinating and important issues.

POSTSCRIPT 3:
DAVID BENATAR REPLIES TO THADDEUS METZ

The dialogue between Professor Metz and me cannot continue indefinitely in this forum – otherwise the debate about one issue would soon exceed the length of our respective interviews. I thus offer only a very brief response to Professor Metz' rejoinder. I do not pretend that it is definitive, but it should make clear what separates his view from mine.

Professor Metz acknowledges that a strong human is not as strong as an elephant and that a mouse does not live as long as a bowhead whale. However, he says that it "seems a leap to conclude that our lives are (in some respect), *bad* for not being as strong as elephants or that the lives of mice are bad for not living as long as whales".

I shall set aside the case of strength, because it introduces complexities best left to a fuller discussion. I focus on length of life. If one thinks that, all things being equal, a longer life is better than a shorter life, then it is a small step, not a leap, to the conclusion that an animal with a shorter life is worse off in that regard than an animal with a longer life. Its shorter life expectancy is indeed unfortunate. The same goes for meaning. If more meaning is, all things being equal, better than less meaning, then it is unfortunate that our lives are much less meaningful than they could be.

Professor Metz seems to think that different interpretations of "could" in the previous sentence would make a difference. He thinks that if something is physically impossible (or even improbable) then it is no cause for regret. This seems to me to be a case of what we might call "optimism-induced existential myopia". By analogy, a human society devoid of all violence is actually (even though not logically) impossible, but it is still reasonable to judge any society against that ideal in determining how violence-free it is. Any violence is unfortunate even if it would be impossible for there to be none.

Turning to Professor Metz's second criticism, I note that he has shifted from his original claim that I am guilty of "incoherence" to saying in his rejoinder that there is a "tension" in my view.

Professor Metz suggests that the tension is this:

1. I judge the meaningfulness of lives from a cosmic standpoint and find them wanting.

2. I do not judge my argument for this conclusion from a cosmic standpoint with regard to the quality of reasoning.

There is, however, no tension here. We have the capacity to view lives from a cosmic perspective – just as we have the capacity to view lives from the perspective of other people. The claim is not that this capacity is infallible, but only that we are able to think about whether lives have meaning from perspectives other than our own.

By contrast, it is impossible for us to judge the quality

of our own reasoning from the perspective of perfect reasoning (if that is what the cosmic perspective would require). We can know *that* our reasoning is imperfect, but we cannot see all the ways in which it would be different if it were perfect.

But recognizing one's fallibility does not mean that one may not reach conclusions – only that one should recognize the possibility of error. Furthermore, the possibility that my conclusion is mistaken is not evidence that it actually is mistaken.

In other words, there is no tension between claiming both:

    1. I can use only those limited tools of reasoning available to me;

and

    2. When I use those tools, I reach the conclusions that it would be better if:
        a. My reasoning tools were more sophisticated; and
        b. My life had cosmic meaning.

There is no tension (or contradiction) because in claiming 1, I am not denying that it would be better if my reasoning tools were more advanced.

ABOUT THE AUTHORS

DAVID BENATAR is Professor of Philosophy at the University of Cape Town in South Africa. His books include *Better Never to Have Been* and *The Human Predicament*.

THADDEUS METZ is Professor of Philosophy at the University of Pretoria in South Africa, and is often credited for having helped develop life's meaning as a distinct field in Anglo-American philosophy over the past 20 years. In addition to numerous professional journal articles, he has published two books on the meaning of life, which are *Meaning in Life: An Analytic Study* (Oxford University Press, 2013) and *God, Soul and the Meaning of Life* (Cambridge University Press, 2019).

JASON WERBELOFF is a science fiction author with a PhD in Philosophy. He has published over a dozen novels, and co-hosts the *Brain in a Vat* Philosophy YouTube channel with Mark Oppenheimer.

MARK OPPENHEIMER studied philosophy at the University of Cape Town. He is a practicing advocate at the Johannesburg Bar, and has appeared in the Supreme Court of Appeal and the Constitutional Court.

Made in the USA
Las Vegas, NV
22 November 2023

81345391R00062